NATURAL DISASTERS

Hurricanes

by Betsy Rathburn

BLASTOFF! READERS
3

BELLWETHER MEDIA • MINNEAPOLIS, MN

Note to Librarians, Teachers, and Parents:

Blastoff! Readers are carefully developed by literacy experts and combine standards-based content with developmentally appropriate text.

Level 1 provides the most support through repetition of high-frequency words, light text, predictable sentence patterns, and strong visual support.

Level 2 offers early readers a bit more challenge through varied simple sentences, increased text load, and less repetition of high-frequency words.

Level 3 advances early-fluent readers toward fluency through increased text and concept load, less reliance on visuals, longer sentences, and more literary language.

Level 4 builds reading stamina by providing more text per page, increased use of punctuation, greater variation in sentence patterns, and increasingly challenging vocabulary.

Level 5 encourages children to move from "learning to read" to "reading to learn" by providing even more text, varied writing styles, and less familiar topics.

Whichever book is right for your reader, Blastoff! Readers are the perfect books to build confidence and encourage a love of reading that will last a lifetime!

This edition first published in 2020 by Bellwether Media, Inc.

No part of this publication may be reproduced in whole or in part without written permission of the publisher. For information regarding permission, write to Bellwether Media, Inc., Attention: Permissions Department, 6012 Blue Circle Drive, Minnetonka, MN 55343.

Library of Congress Cataloging-in-Publication Data

Names: Rathburn, Betsy, author.
Title: Hurricanes / by Betsy Rathburn.
Description: Minneapolis, MN : Bellwether Media, Inc., 2020. | Series:
  Blastoff! Readers. Natural Disasters | Audience: Ages 5-8. | Audience: K
  to grade 3. | Includes bibliographical references and index.
Identifiers: LCCN 2019001503 (print) | LCCN 2019003088 (ebook) | ISBN
  9781618915672 (ebook) | ISBN 9781644870266 (hardcover : alk. paper) | ISBN
  9781618917478 (pbk. : alk. paper)
Subjects: LCSH: Hurricanes--Juvenile literature.
Classification: LCC QC944.2 (ebook) | LCC QC944.2 .R376 2020 (print) | DDC
  551.55/2--dc23
LC record available at https://lccn.loc.gov/2019001503

Editor: Al Albertson   Designer: Josh Brink

Printed in the United States of America, North Mankato, MN

Table of Contents

What Are Hurricanes?   4

How Do Hurricanes Form?   6

Hurricane Damage   10

Predicting Disaster   16

Glossary   22

To Learn More   23

Index   24

What Are Hurricanes?

Hurricanes are powerful storms. They are sometimes called **tropical cyclones**.

These huge storms start in **tropical** oceans. In the United States, they bring disaster to eastern coastal areas.

How Many Hurricanes?

How many hurricanes happen across the United States every year?

N
W · E
S

0 hurricanes per year = ☐
1 to 28 hurricanes per year = ☐
29 to 64 hurricanes per year = ☐
65 to 141 hurricanes per year = ☐

How Do Hurricanes Form?

Hurricanes form when warm air rises over ocean water. The rising air gathers **moisture**. It leaves behind a pocket of cold air. This air rises, too.

As the air continues to rise, clouds form over the ocean.

eye

Wind causes the clouds to spin. A calm **eye** forms in the center of the spinning clouds.

Beyond the **eye wall**, outer clouds spin fast. Hurricanes have wind speeds of at least 74 miles (119 kilometers) per hour!

How Hurricanes Form

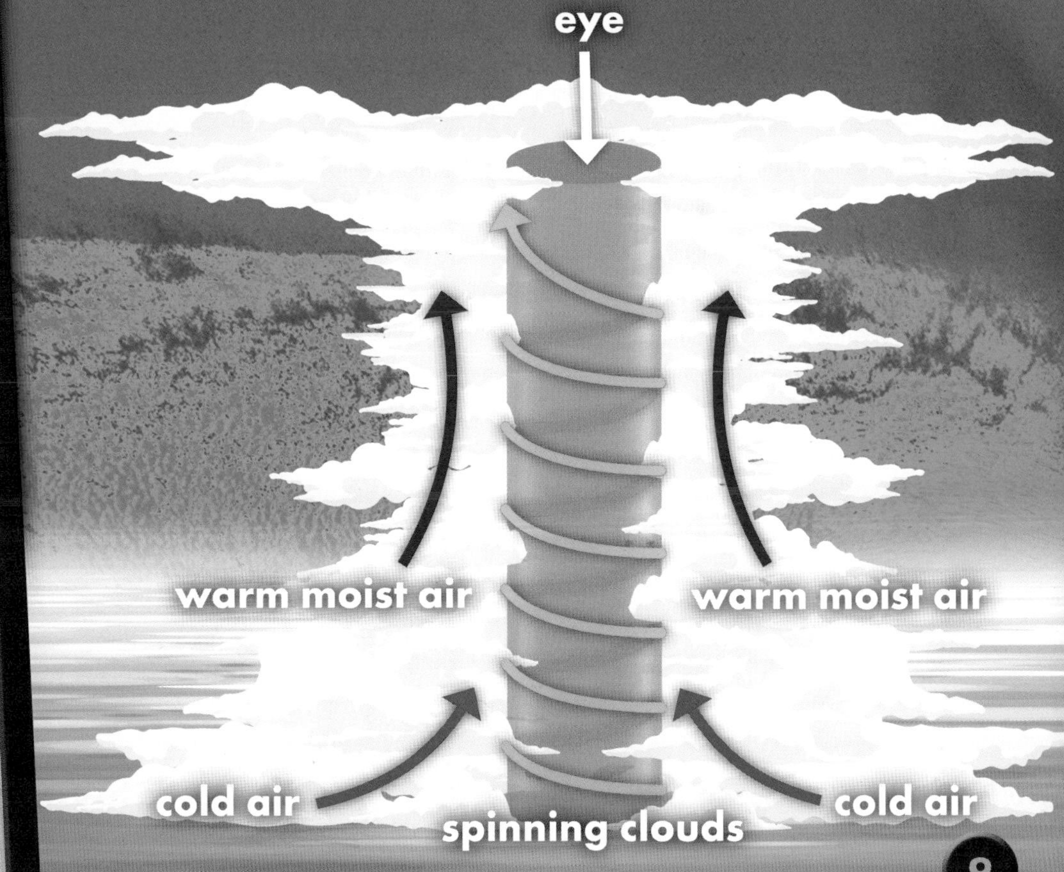

eye

warm moist air

warm moist air

cold air

spinning clouds

cold air

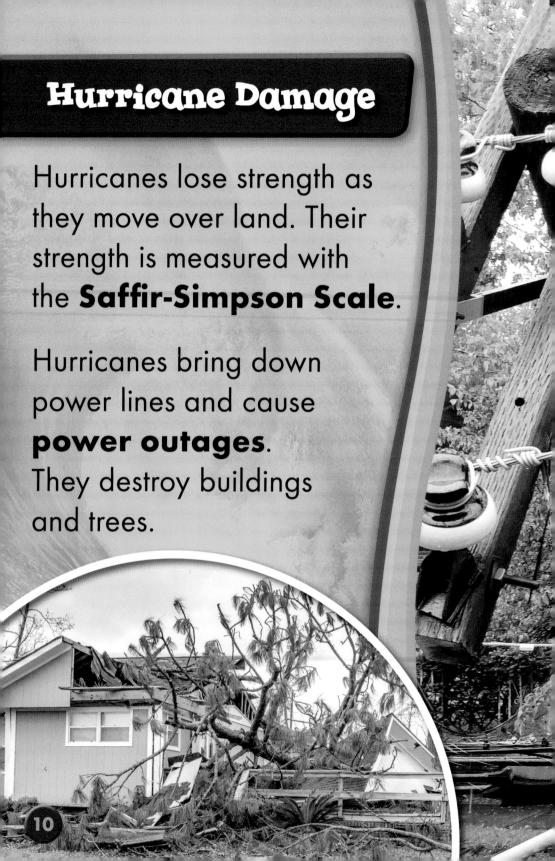

Hurricane Damage

Hurricanes lose strength as they move over land. Their strength is measured with the **Saffir-Simpson Scale**.

Hurricanes bring down power lines and cause **power outages**. They destroy buildings and trees.

Saffir-Simpson Scale

Category 1: winds 74 to 95 miles
(119 to 153 kilometers) per hour
- storm surges up to 5 feet (1.5 meters)
- minor flooding and damage

Category 2: winds 96 to 110 miles
(154 to 177 kilometers) per hour
- storm surges up to 8 feet (2 meters)
- some flooding and damage

Category 3: winds 111 to 129 miles
(179 to 208 kilometers) per hour
- storm surges up to 12 feet (4 meters)
- serious flooding and damage

Category 4: winds 131 to 156 miles
(209 to 251 kilometers) per hour
- storm surges up to 18 feet (5 meters)
- mobile homes completely destroyed

Category 5: winds more than 157 miles
(253 kilometers) per hour
- storm surges more than 18 feet (5 meters)
- small and large buildings destroyed

downed
power line

storm surge

Winds also push huge waves of water onto land. These **storm surges** can be more than 20 feet (6 meters) tall!

Storm surges bring the most danger to people in old, weak houses. Low areas near the coast are also in danger.

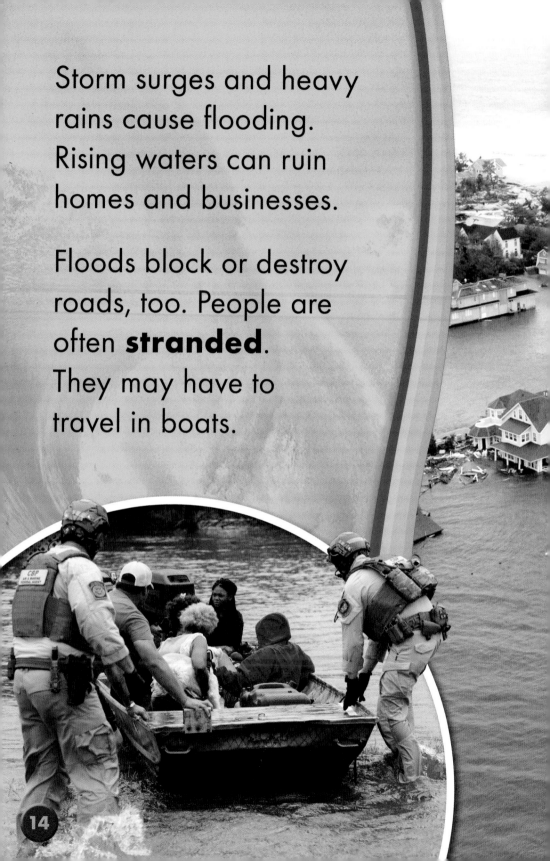

Storm surges and heavy rains cause flooding. Rising waters can ruin homes and businesses.

Floods block or destroy roads, too. People are often **stranded**. They may have to travel in boats.

flooding

Predicting Disaster

meteorologist

Hurricane season lasts from May through November. But **meteorologists** make **predictions** before the season begins.

They look at **climate** information from past hurricane seasons. This helps **forecast** future hurricane activity.

Meteorologists look for patterns in the paths of past hurricanes. They create **models** that help predict future hurricane paths.

Predictions help keep people safe!

path of Hurricane Katrina

Hurricane Profile

Name: Hurricane Katrina

Dates: August 23 to August 31, 2005

Location: the southern United States, especially New Orleans, Louisiana

Category: Category 5

Damage to Property:
- more than 200,000 homes destroyed
- thousands of businesses destroyed
- at least $100 billion in damage

Damage to People:
- millions of people evacuated
- thousands of jobs lost
- thousands missed or left school

Hurricane Katrina damage

People usually have time to prepare for hurricanes. They stock up on food and gas. They also board up windows.

evacuation

Many people **evacuate** before powerful hurricanes. When hurricanes strike, it is best to be far from the coast!

Glossary

climate—the usual temperature, precipitation, and other weather conditions of an area

evacuate—to leave a dangerous area

eye—the low-pressure center of a hurricane

eye wall—the wall of clouds around a hurricane's eye

forecast—to predict future weather events

meteorologists—scientists who study weather

models—systems of data used to predict the weather

moisture—water or other liquid

power outages—events in which no electricity is available

predictions—guesses based on collected information

Saffir-Simpson Scale—a scale used to measure the strength of hurricanes from Category 1 to Category 5

storm surges—events in which hurricane winds push ocean water to shore

stranded—left behind with no way of escape

tropical—related to the tropics; the tropics is a hot, rainy region near the equator.

tropical cyclones—rotating masses of air that begin in the tropics

To Learn More

AT THE LIBRARY

Gagliardi, Sue. *Hurricane Katrina*. Lake Elmo, Minn.: Focus Readers, 2020.

Meinking, Mary. *Natural Disasters*. Minneapolis, Minn.: Pop!, 2019.

Perish, Patrick. *Survive a Hurricane*. Minneapolis, Minn.: Bellwether Media, 2017.

ON THE WEB

FACTSURFER

Factsurfer.com gives you a safe, fun way to find more information.

1. Go to www.factsurfer.com.

2. Enter "hurricanes" into the search box and click 🔍.

3. Select your book cover to see a list of related web sites.

Index

air, 6, 7

boats, 14

buildings, 10

businesses, 14

climate, 17

clouds, 7, 8, 9

coastal areas, 5, 13, 21

evacuate, 21

eye, 8

eye wall, 9

flooding, 14, 15

forecast, 17

formation, 6, 7, 8, 9

houses, 13, 14

Hurricane Katrina, 18, 19

hurricane season, 16, 17

land, 10, 12

meteorologists, 16, 17, 18

models, 18

moisture, 6

oceans, 5, 6, 7

paths, 18

power lines, 10, 11

power outages, 10

predictions, 16, 18

prepare, 20

roads, 14

Saffir-Simpson Scale, 10, 11

storm surges, 12, 13, 14

travel, 14

trees, 10

tropical cyclones, 4

United States, 5

wind, 8, 9, 12

The images in this book are reproduced through the courtesy of: Gennady Stetsenko, cover (hero); andrey polivanov, cover (water); Photobank gallery, cover (trees); FotoKina, pp. 2-3, 4; Drew McArthur, p. 6; Charlie Blacker/ Alamy, p. 7; Vladi333, p. 8; Terry Kelly, p. 10; ungvar, p. 11; Mike Newman/ Alamy, p. 12; Bob Pool, p. 13; CBP Photo/ Alamy, p. 14; age fotostock/ Alamy, p. 17; Dennis Hallinan/ Alamy, p. 18; Marc Pagani Photography, p. 19; Mia2you, p. 20; ZUMA Press, Inc/ Alamy, p. 21.